Pond
Life
Paper Quilling Projects

Dana Woodard

All of the step-by-step photographs in this publication were taken by and feature the author, Dana Woodard, demonstrating how to create each project. No other models were used.

Front cover: background paper used from the Safari Chic Stack textured card stock collection by DCWV
www.diecutswithaview.com

DEDICATION

This book is dedicated to Moira Hiscock who inspired me and encouraged me to write this book. She took the time to go over each pattern and gave me the perspective I needed to see these with a fresh set of eyes. She had a personal say in each and every one of these quilling patterns, as well as others that I plan to put in future books. She challenged me to do better and I made many revisions on the patterns when she would say to me "too fiddly!" It is my regret that she never got to see the final completion of this book.. She was a teacher, a mentor, a friend, and the mother -in-law I never had. She will be greatly missed. This one's for you "mom".

CONTENTS

Leap Frogs

Level - Easy

You Will Need:

- 1 strip of green 1/8" (3 mm) quilling paper, 8 inches (20 cm) long
- 1 strip of green 1/8" (3 mm) quilling paper, 12 inches (30.5 cm) long
- 2 strips of green 1/8" (3 mm) quilling paper, 1 ½ inch (4 cm) long
- 2 strips of green 1/8" (3 mm) quilling paper, ½ inch (1.5 cm) long
- 2 strips of green 1/8" (3 mm) quilling paper, 1 inch (2.5 cm) long
- 1 strip of yellow 1/8" (3 mm) quilling paper, 3 inches (7.5 cm) long

Directions:

Making The Head:

1. Roll and glue the 8 inch green strip into a loose coil.

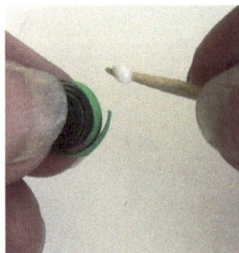

2. Glue the end down so that it does not unravel.

3. Flatten one end of the coil so that you now have a semi-circle.

Making The Body:

1. Roll the 12 inch green strip into a loose coil and glue the end down so that it does not unravel.

2. Flatten one end of the coil so that you now have a semi-circle.

3. Slightly pinch the sides of the semi-circle together so the shape is more oval and looks like a door.

4. Glue the flat edge of one semi-circle to the flat edge of the door shape. Set it aside.

Making The Back Legs:

1. To make the back legs, take one of the 1 ½ inch green strips and fold just the tip of it over.

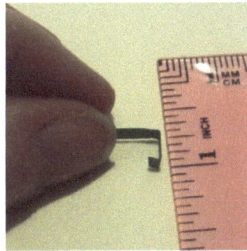

2. Make another fold in the same direction about ¼ of an inch above the first fold.

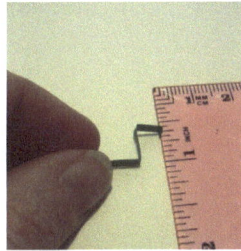

3. Make a third fold in the opposite direction about ½ of an inch above that.

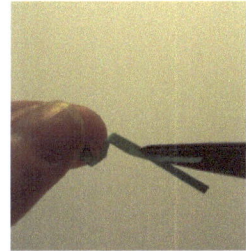

4. On the long end with no folds, take a pair of scissors and cut lengthwise up the strip. Cut almost to the last fold but leave about 3/8 ths of an inch of space before you get to the fold.

5. Roll each side of the cut strip in a loose coil in the opposite direction of each other.

6. Take one of the ½ inch green strips and cut it length wise up the middle.

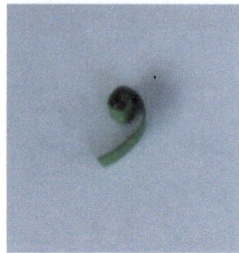

7. Roll one of the cut pieces into an open ended loose coil. Glue the newly rolled loose coil to the back of one the two coils on the leg.

8. This is the middle toe and it should be sitting slightly taller than the other two. Repeat steps 1 – 8 for the second back leg.

Making The Front Legs:

1. To make the front leg, take one of the 1 inch green strips and fold just the tip of it over.

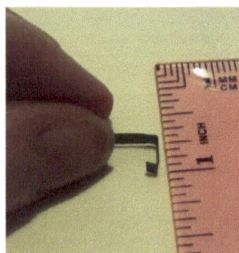

2. Make another fold in the same direction about ¼ of an inch above the first fold.

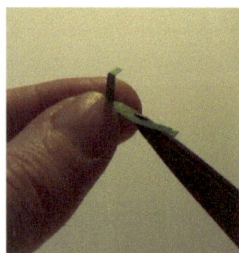

3. Cut lengthwise up the strip almost to the second fold, but stop about 3/8ths of an inch before you get to it.

4. Roll each side of the cut strip in a loose coil in the opposite direction of each other.

5. *Take one of the ½ inch green strip that you had cut earlier and roll it into an open ended loose coil.*

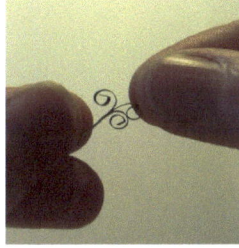

6. *Glue the newly rolled loose coil to the back of one the two coils on the leg. This is also a middle toe and it should be sitting slightly taller that the other two.*

7. *Repeat steps 1 to 6 to make the second front leg.*

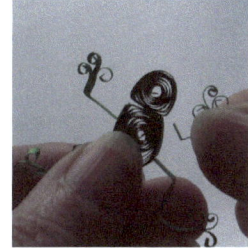

8. *Glue the front and back legs onto the body.*

Making The Eyes:

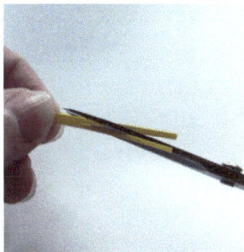

1. *Take one of the 3 inch yellow strips and cut it length wise up the middle.*

2. *Roll one of the newly cut yellow strips into a tight coil.*

3. *Glue the end so that the coil does not unravel.*

Optional steps 4a - 4c : To make the eyes look a larger and as though they have more of a whimsical stare, do the following:

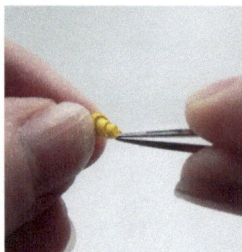

4a. *Take a pair of tweezers and pull the middle of the coil out from the center a little bit.*

4b. *Cut off the yellow piece that you have pulled from the center.*

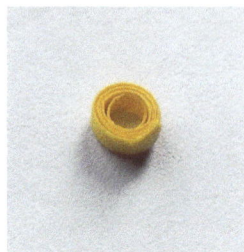

4c. *You should now have a circle with an open center.*

5. *Glue the yellow eyes to the frogs head.*

6. *Repeat steps 1 to 5 to make the second eye.*

You now have a Leap Frog! Create more and you can have them jumping all over your projects!

Leaping Lizards

Level – Easy

You Will Need:

- 1 strip of green 1/8" (3 mm) quilling paper, 8 inches (20.5 cm) long
- 1 strip of green 1/8" (3 mm) quilling paper, 12 inches (30.5 cm) long
- 4 strips of green 1/8" (3 mm) quilling paper, 1 inch (2.5 cm) long
- 2 strips of green 1/8" (3 mm) quilling paper, ½ inch (1.5 cm) long
- 1 strip of yellow 1/8" (3 mm) quilling paper, 3 inches (7.5 cm) long
- 1 strip of green 1/8" (3 mm) quilling paper, 1 ¼ inches (3.5 cm) long

Directions:

Making The Head:

1. Roll and glue the 8 inch green strip into a loose coil. Glue the end.

2. Pinch one end of the coil so that you now have a tear drop shape.

Making The Body:

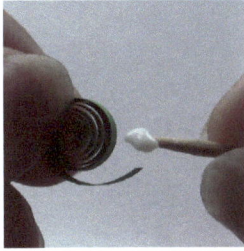

1. Roll the 12 inch green strip into a loose coil and glue the end.

2. Pinch both ends of the coil so that you now have an eye shape. Glue the round end of the tear drop shape to one of the flat sides of the eye shape.

3. It will sit up close to the tip, but not directly on it so that it will look like the head is off on an angle. Set it aside.

Making The Legs:

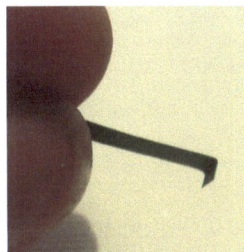

1. To make the legs, take one of the 1 inch green strips and fold just the tip of it over.

2. Cut lengthwise up the strip, stopping about half way up.

3. Roll each side of the cut strip in a loose coil in the opposite direction of each other.

4. Now take one of the ½ inch green strips and cut it length wise up the middle.

5. Roll one of the cut pieces into an open ended loose coil.

6. Glue the newly rolled loose coil to the back of one the two coils on the leg in such a way that it is sitting in the middle as the middle toe.

7. Glue the leg onto the body.

8. Repeat steps 1 – 7 to add the second, third and fourth legs to the lizard.

Making The Tail:

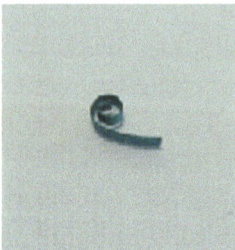

1. Take the 1 and ¼ inch green strip and roll one end of it into an open ended loose coil.

2. At the other end make a slight curve that goes in the opposite direction. This is the tail.

3. Glue the tail to the body of the lizard.

Making The Eyes:

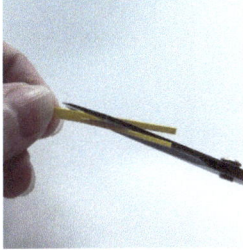

1. Take one of the 3 inch yellow strips and cut it length wise up the middle.

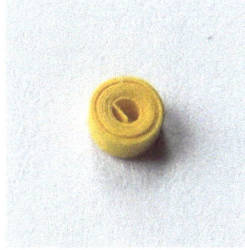

2. Drawing 1: Roll one of the newly cut yellow strips into a tight coil.

3. Glue the end so that the coil does not unravel.

Optional steps 4a - 4c : To make the eyes look a larger and as though they have more of a whimsical stare, do the following:

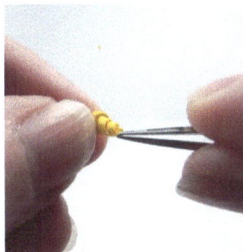

4a. Take a pair of tweezers and pull the middle of the coil out from the center a little bit.

4b. Cut off the yellow piece that you have pulled from the center.

4c. You should now have a circle with an open center.

5. *Glue the yellow eye to the lizards head.*

6. *Repeat steps 1 to 5 to add the second eye.*

You now have a Leaping Lizard! Create more and you can have them leap off your pages!

Snail (Flat Version)

Level - Easy

You Will Need:

- 1 strip of dark brown 1/8" quilling paper, 8 inches (20.5 cm) long
- 1 strip of light brown 1/8" quilling paper, 9 inches (23 cm) long
- 1 strip of light brown 1/8" quilling paper, 1 ¼ inches (3 cm) long

Directions:

Making The Body/Tail:

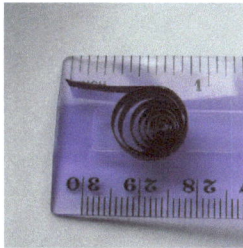

1. Roll the 8 inch dark brown strip into a loose coil, leaving about a half of an inch tail on the end of it.

2. Glue it so that your coil does not come undone.

3. With your fingers, carefully pinch the coil very gently about ¼ inch away from where the tail starts giving the one end a slight corner to it.

**Tip: Don't pinch the corner too hard because you don't want the corner to be too pronounced. It should have just a gentle curve and barely noticeable angle to it.

Making The Head:

1. *Take the 9 inch light brown strip and roll it into a tight coil leaving a tail of unrolled paper about an inch long. The tail of unrolled paper will be the antennae.*

2. *Add a dab of glue at the base of the antennae to keep it in place.*

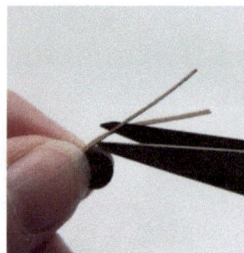

3. *Cut the tail piece of the antennae length wise, straight down the middle, being careful not to cut them right off.*

4. *Curl each of the two antennae pieces leaving one just a bit higher than the other. Your head is finished.*

** Tip: If you wish to have a bigger head for the snail, try using a 12inch (30.5 cm) strip instead of the 9 inch strip.

Adding The Head To The Body:

1. *Glue the head to the shell about a ¼ inch above where you pinched the slight corner.*

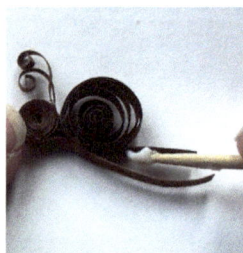

2. *Take the 1 ¼ inch strip of light brown and glue it just below the head all along the base of the tail so that it forms a bit of a neck on the snail. This also helps to strengthen the tail by making it a bit thicker.*

3. *If needed, trim up the tail just a little.*

18

You now have a little snail! You can use him to decorate gifts or cards!

Snail

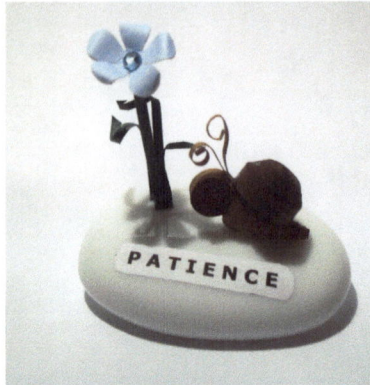

Level – Intermediate

You Will Need:

- 1 strip of dark brown 1/8" quilling paper, 24 inches (61 cm) long
- 1 strip of light brown 1/8" quilling paper, 9 inches (23 cm) long
- 1 strip of light brown 1/8" quilling paper, 6 inches (15.5 cm) long

Directions:

Making The Shell:

**Tip: If you don't have a strip that is long enough, just glue two together so that it makes one long strip of 24 inches and roll that.*

1. Roll the 24 inch brown strip into a tight solid coil.

2. Glue the end so that your coil does not come undone.

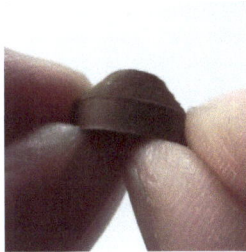

3. With your fingers, carefully push the center of the brown coil out until it forms a dome. This will be your shell.

4. Coat the inner side of the dome with glue so that it won't fall apart.

5. Set it aside and let it dry. It should look like a little dome.

Making The Head:

1. Take the 9 inch light brown strip and roll it into a tight coil leaving a tail of unrolled paper about an inch long. The tail of unrolled paper will be the antennae.

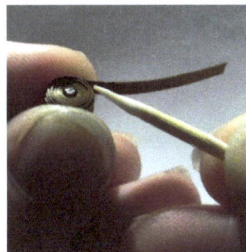

2. Add a dab of glue at the base of the antennae to keep it in place.

3. Cut the tail piece of the antennae length wise, straight down the middle, being careful not to cut them right off.

4. Curl each of the two antennae pieces leaving one just a bit higher than the other. Your head is finished. Set it aside.

** Tip: If you wish to have a bigger head for the snail, try using a 12inch (30.5 cm) strip instead of the 9 inch strip.

21

Making The Body:

Now this is where it gets a little tricky. You will need to be like the snail and have some patience with this part. It may take a couple of tries before you get the hang of it, but eventually you will have the body of a snail.

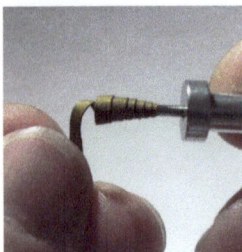

1. Take the 6 inch strip of light brown and start to roll it into a cone shape. As it gets longer the cone will start to naturally curve a little bit. That is OK, it is supposed to do that.

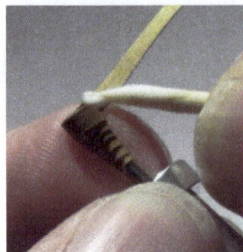

2. Be sure to glue it at almost every turn you make or it will quickly come apart on you.

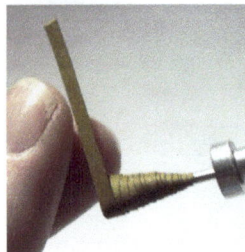

3. Continue to roll and glue until you have only about an inch or so of paper left then stop and make sure everything is glued up to that point.

4. Now fold the end over the opening so that it starts to cover the opening, making it narrower. It will not fully cover the opening, but it doesn't need to.

5. Glue the piece that you have just folded over to the edge on the opposite side of the cone.

6. Cut off any excess paper that remains.

7. You should now have a shape that resembles something like an odd shaped ice cream cone with an oval shaped opening.

8. Coat the inner side of the cone along the top edge with glue so that you can attach the head.

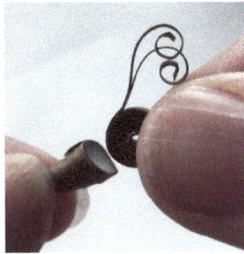

9. Glue the head into the opening of the cone shaped body.

10. The head will be turned to the side somewhat and will not sit perfectly straight, but that's OK. It gives the snail some character and will not be that noticeable. Let it dry for a couple of minutes before trying to attach the shell.

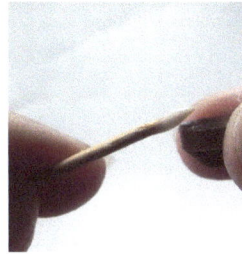

11. Add some glue to two opposite ends of the underside of the snails shell where it will touch the body.

12. Attach the shell to the body and head. The edge of the shell should sit up right where the head and the body meet.

You now have a little snail! Great for decorating paper weights, magnets or making jewellry!

Mallard Duck

Level – Easy

You Will Need:

- 1 strip of black 1/8" quilling paper, 1 ¼ inch (3 cm) long
- 1 strips of white 1/8" quilling paper, 2 inches (5 cm) long
- 1 strip of dark green 1/8" quilling paper, 18 inches (46 cm) long
- 1 strip of yellow 1/8" quilling paper, 1 ½ inches (4 cm) long
- 1 strips of white 1/8" quilling paper, 4 inches (10 cm) long
- 1 strips of medium brown 1/8" quilling paper, 12 inches (30.5 cm) long
- 2 strips of grey 1/8" quilling paper, 10 inches (20.5 cm) long

Directions:

Making The Head:

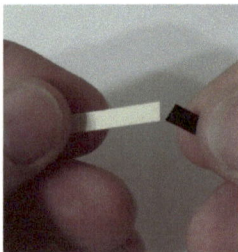

1. Take the black 1 ¼ inch strip and glue the end of it to the white 2 inch strip.

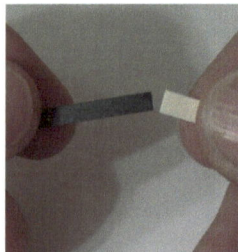

2. Take the dark green 18 inch strip and glue the end of it to the other end of the 2 inch white strip.

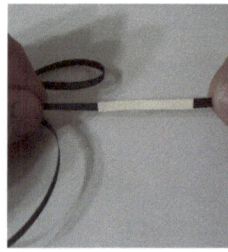

3. You should now have one long strip going from black to white to green.

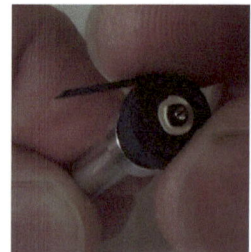

4. Starting with the black end, roll that strip into a tight coil and glue the end so that it does not unravel.

24

Making The Beak:

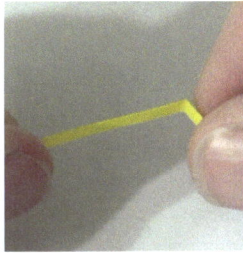

1. Take the strip of yellow paper and make a fold at one end at about the 1/8th inch (3 mm) point.

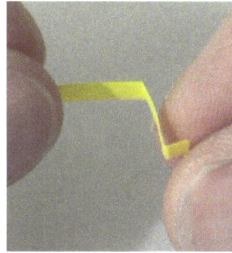

2. Make a second fold in the opposite direction about 5/16th inch (8 mm) from the first fold.

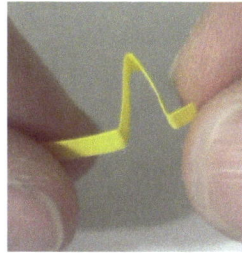

3. Make a third fold in the opposite direction about 5/16th inch (8 mm) from the second fold.

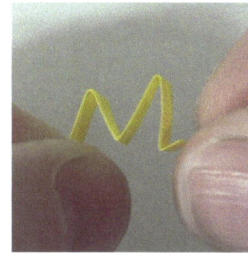

4. Make a fourth fold in the opposite direction about ¼ inch (7 mm) from the third fold.

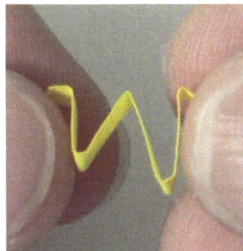

5. Make a fifth and final fold in the opposite direction about 1/8th inch (3 mm) from the fourth fold.

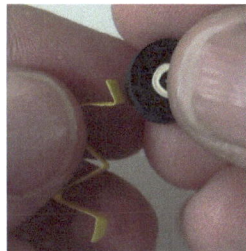

6. Glue the end where the first fold of the yellow strip is to the head where you would like your beak to be.

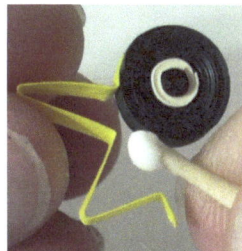

7. Glue the third fold to the head directly underneath where you have glued the first fold.

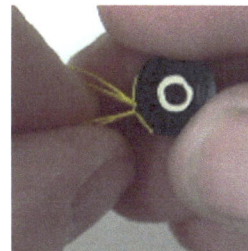

8. Glue the end of the yellow strip where the fifth fold is to the head directly underneath the third fold.

25

Making The Neck:

1. Take the 4 inch white strip and roll it into a tight coil.

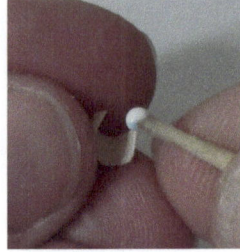

2. Glue the end so that your coil does not come undone.

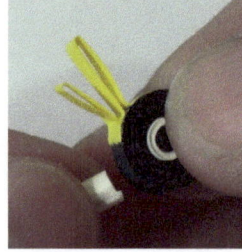

3. Glue the white coil to the under side of the head.

4. Set it aside to dry.

Making The Body And Wings:

1. Take the 12 inch strip of medium brown and roll it into a loose coil. Glue the end so that it is a closed coil.

2. Pinch one end of the coil so that it forms a tear drop shape. This is the body.

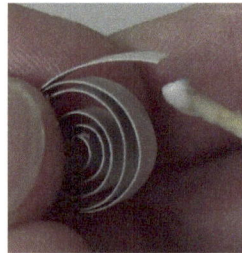

3. Take one of the 10 inch strips of grey paper and roll it into a loose coil. Glue the end so that it is a closed coil.

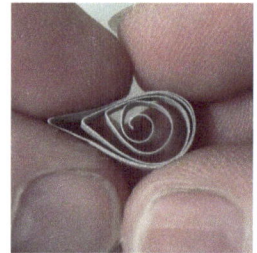

4. Pinch one end of the coil so that it forms a tear drop shape. This is your first wing.

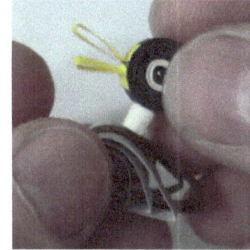

5. Take the second 10 inch strips of grey paper and also roll it into a loose coil. Glue the end so that it is a closed coil.

6. Pinch one end of the coil so that it forms a tear drop shape. This is the second wing.

7. Glue one of the grey tear drop shapes to one side of the medium brown tear drop shape, making sure that the round edges match up. Repeat step seven for the second grey tear drop shape on the opposite side of the body.

8. Glue the head to the body, making sure that it is sitting back on the body a bit so that the duck doesn't fall forward flat on his beak.

You now have a little mallard duck! He will be great for Father's Day projects or projects for bird lovers!

OPTIONAL:

If you wish to use this design on a greeting card, only use one wing instead of two and only use 8 inches of paper for the wing instead of 10.

Loon

Level – Easy

You Will Need:

- 1 strip of red 1/8" quilling paper, 2 inch (5 cm) long
- 1 strip of black 1/8" quilling paper, 18 inches (46 cm) long
- 1 strip of grey 1/8" quilling paper, 1 inch (2.5 cm) long
- 1 strip of white 1/8" quilling paper, 4 inches (10 cm) long
- 1 strip of black 1/8" quilling paper, ¾ inch (2 cm) long
- 1 strip of white 1/8" quilling paper, 12 inches (30.5 cm) long
- 1 strip of black 1/8" quilling paper, 1 ½ inches (4 cm) long
- 2 strips of black 1/8" quilling paper, 10 inches (25.5 cm) long
- 1 strip of white 1/8" quilling paper, ½ inch (1.5 cm) long
- A pair of tweezers

Directions:

Making The Head:

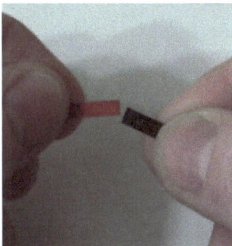

1. Take the red 2 inch strip and glue the end of it to the black 18 inch strip.

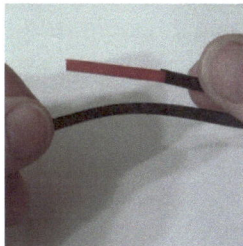

2. You should now have one long strip going from red to black.

3. Roll that strip into a tight coil.

4. Glue the end in place so it does not unravel on you.

Making The Beak:

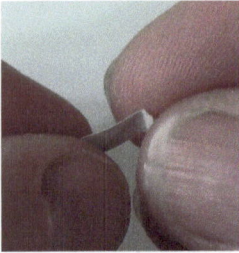

1. Take the strip of grey paper and make a fold at one end about 1/16th inch (2mm) long.

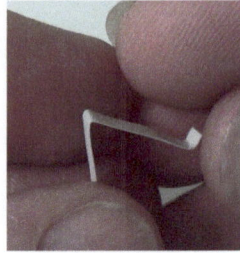

2. Make a second fold in the opposite direction about ½ inch (12 mm) from the first fold.

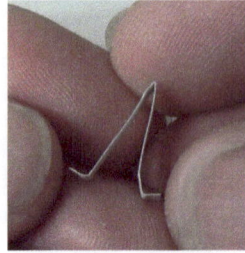

3. Make a third fold in the opposite direction about ½ inch (12 mm) from the second fold.

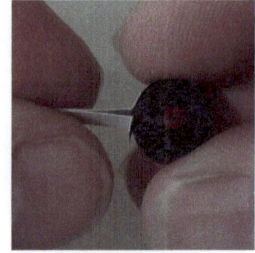

4. Glue the end of the first and third fold of the grey strip to the head where you would like your beak to be.

Making The Neck:

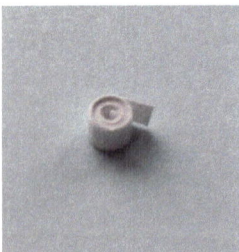

1. Take the 4 inch white strip and roll it into a tight coil.

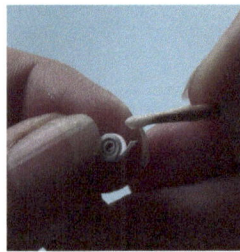

2. Glue the end so that your coil does not come undone.

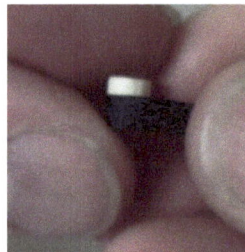

3. Take the ¾ inch black strip and glue it around the bottom edge of the white coil. Trim off any excess you may have.

4. Glue the white and black tube shape to the under side of the head with the white side up and then set it aside to dry.

Making The Body:

1. Take the 12 inch strip of white and roll it into a loose coil.

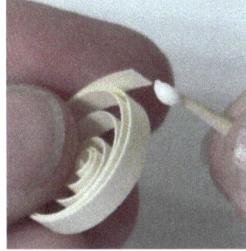

2. Glue the end so that it is a closed coil.

3. Pinch one end of the coil so that it forms a tear drop shape. This is the body.

4. Take the 1 ½ inch black strip and wrap it around the body starting from the middle of one side, going over the point and ending in the middle of the other side.

Making The Wings:

1. Take one of the 10 inch strips of black paper and roll it into a loose coil. Glue the end so that it is a closed coil.

2. Pinch one end of the coil so that it forms a tear drop shape. This is your first wing.

3. Take the second 10 inch strip of black paper and also roll it into a loose coil. Glue the end so that it is a closed coil.

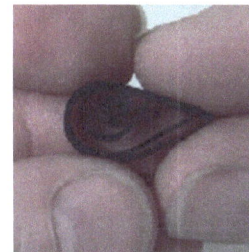

4. Pinch one end of the coil so that it forms a tear drop shape. This is the second wing.

5. Glue one of the black tear drop shapes to one side of the body, making sure that the round edges match up. Repeat for the second black tear drop shape on the opposite side of the body.

6. Glue the head to the body, making sure that it is sitting back on the body a bit so that the loon doesn't fall over forward flat on his beak.

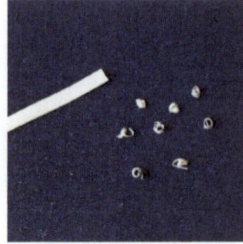

7. Loons have spots on their backs so take one of the white ½ strips and cut about 8 tiny circles to use as spots.

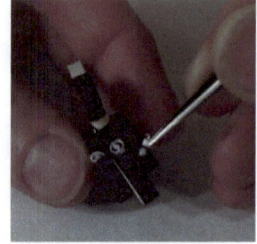

8. One by one, glue each of the tiny white spots to the back of the loon using a pair of tweezers. If you find eight to be too many, try using only 6 spots.

Your loon is now ready to swim around in your pond! You can use it as a three dimensional decoration or leave one of the wings off and you can use it to decorate a greeting card.

OPTIONAL:

If you wish to use this design on a greeting card, only use one wing instead of two and only use 8 inches of paper for the wing instead of 10. Instead of trying to curl the white pieces for the spots, just cut up some tiny pieces of white paper and glue them on.

Cat Tails

Level - Advanced

You Will Need:

- 3 strips of medium brown 1/8" quilling paper, 3 ½ inches (9 cm) long
- 1 strips of green 1/8" quilling paper, 3/8 inch (1 cm) long
- 1 strips of green 1/8" quilling paper, 6 ½ inches (16.5 cm) long
- 1 strips of green 1/8" quilling paper, 1 ¾ inches (4.5 cm) long
- 1 strips of green 1/8" quilling paper, 1 ¼ inches (3 cm) long
- 1 strips of blue 1/8" quilling paper, 6 inches (15.5 cm) long
- A round tooth pick

Directions:

Making The Flower Head And Spike:

1. Roll the first 3 ½ inch medium brown strip into a tight solid coil. The coil should be about 3/8 inch (½ cm) in diameter.

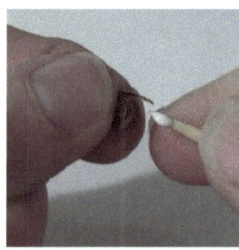

2. Glue the end so that your coil does not come undone.

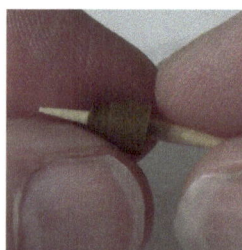

3. With your quilling tool or a tooth pick, carefully push the center of the coil out until it forms a dome with a bit of a hole in the center.

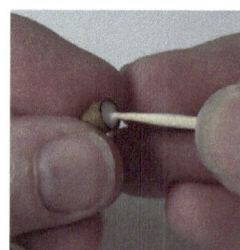

4. Coat the inner side of the dome with glue so that it won't fall apart.

5. Roll the second 3 ½ inch medium brown strip into a tight solid coil, also making sure to glue the end so the coil does not come undone. This coil should also be about 3/8 inch (½ cm) in diameter.

6. Glue the second coil to the underside of the dome.

7. Roll the third 3 ½ inch medium brown strip into a tight solid coil. This coil should also be about 3/8 inch (½ cm) in diameter.

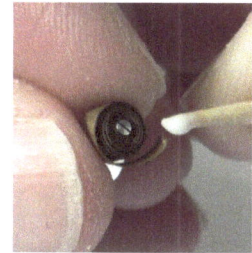

8. Again, glue the end so that your coil does not come undone.

9. With your quilling tool or tooth pick, carefully push the center of the medium brown coil out until it forms a dome.

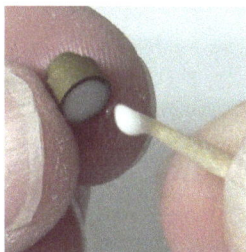

10. Coat the inner side of the dome with glue so that it won't fall apart.

11. Glue the underside of the third coil to the flat part of the second coil.

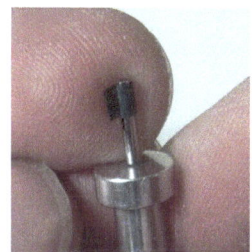

12. Take the green 3/8 inch long strip and roll it into a tube shape.

13. Glue the end so that your tube does not come undone.

14. Glue the green tube to the top of the brown dome with the hole in the center.

15. This is the flower head of the cat tail. Set it aside to dry while you work on the stalk.

Making The Stalk:

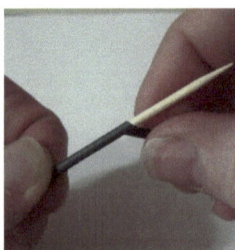

1. Take your round tooth pick and wrap the 6 ½ inch green paper around it to form a tube roughly 1 ½ inches long. Leave a 1 ½ inch long tail of paper unrolled.

2. When it is wrapped, coat the whole tube with glue and let it dry. Be sure that you don't accidentally glue it right to the toothpick and that it will slide off of your toothpick when you are done.

3. Take unrolled 1 ½ inch long tail of paper and cut it on a diagonal angle so that it comes to a point.

4. Wrap the tail half way around the stalk once. Then make loose and gentle curls in the tail so that it looks like a spiraling leaf.

Making The Leaves:

1. Take the 1 ¾ inches green strip and cut it on a diagonal angle so that it comes to a point.

2. Glue the uncut edge just above where the first leaf started.

3. Make loose and gentle curls in it so that it also looks like a spiraling leaf. Try to get the leaf to go in the opposite direction of the first one.

4. Take 1 ¼ inch strip of green and cut it on a diagonal angle so that it comes to a point.

5. Glue the uncut edge just above both of the other leaves.

6. Make loose and gentle curve in it so that it also looks like a spiraling leaf.

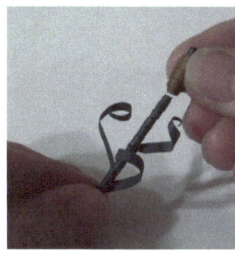

7. Glue the cat tail head onto the stalk.

1. To get the cat tail to stand up on it's own you will need to use the blue 6 inch strip of paper and roll it into a coil with an open center.

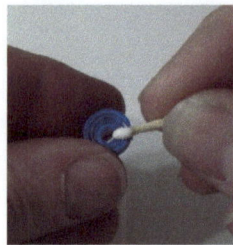

2. Coat the under side of the blue coil with glue and let it dry for a few minutes.

3. Once it is dry, glue the cat tail into the open center of the blue coil.

Tip: If you find that your cat tail is still not standing up properly after gluing it to the blue coil, try either 1) adding additional blue coils and gluing them to the side of the first one for added balance, or 2) try adding another strip of blue paper to the original coil and wrap it around to make the coil larger, or 3) make multiple cat tails and glue all the water bases together.

You now have a cat tail to begin your pond with! Make as many as you would like to give your pond plenty of plant life for your quilled insects, birds and animals to live in, sit on and hide behind.

Blue Heron

Level - Advanced

You Will Need:

- 1 strip of black 1/8" quilling paper, 1 ¼ inch (3 cm) long

- 1 strips of yellow 1/8" quilling paper, 3 inches (8 cm) long

- 1 strip of grey 1/8" quilling paper, 19 inches (48 cm) long

- 1 strip of black 1/8" quilling paper, 1 inch (2.5 cm) long

- 1 strips of beige 1/8" quilling paper, 2 ½ inches (6.5 cm) long

- 1 strips of grey 1/8" quilling paper, 7 inch (18 cm) long

- 1 strips of grey 1/8" quilling paper, 18 inches (46 cm) long

- 2 strips of blue-grey 1/8" quilling paper, 10 inches (25.5 cm) long

- 1 strips of grey 1/8" quilling paper, 1 inches (2.5 cm) long

- 2 strips of grey 1/8" quilling paper, ½ inch (1.5 cm) long

- 2 strips of yellow 1/8" quilling paper, 5 ½ inches (114 cm) long

- 6 strips of blue 1/8" quilling paper, 6 inches (15.5 cm) long

- A round tooth pick

Making The Head:

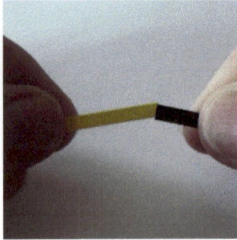

1. Take the black 1 ¼ inch strip and glue the end of it to the yellow 3 inch strip.

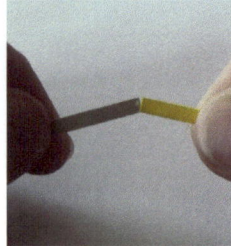

2. Take the grey 19 inch strip and glue the end of it to the other end of the 3 inch yellow strip.

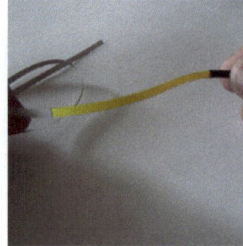

3. You should now have one long strip going from black to yellow to grey.

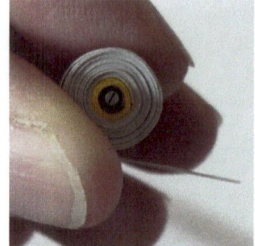

4. Starting with the black end, roll that strip into a tight coil and glue it so that it won't come undone.

5. Take the black 1 inch strip and glue half of it onto the tight coil where you want the top of the head to be.

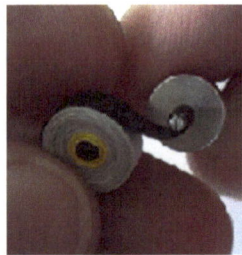

6. Curl the part that you didn't glue to the head in an upwards direction.

7. Cut the curled part length wise up the middle so that you have two curled sections.

8. Separate the two curled sections a little bit so that one is slightly lower than the other.

Making The Beak :

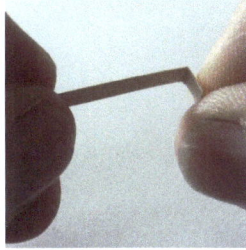

1. Take the strip of beige paper and make a fold at one end about 1/8th inch (3mm) long.

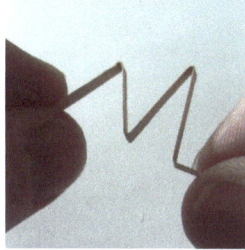

2. Make more folds in the opposite direction so that it forms a W shape.

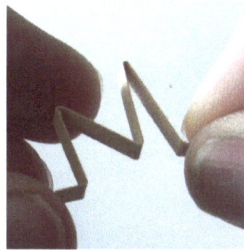

3. Make a final fold in the opposite direction about 1/8th inch (3mm) from the other end. It will look something like a W with wings. This is the beak.

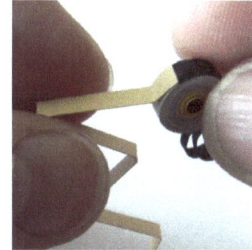

4. Start by gluing one end of the beak to the head directly underneath the black strip on the head.

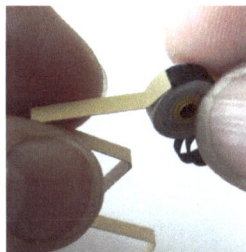

5. Continue to glue all the points of the beak to the head until the beak is complete.

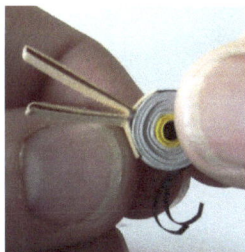

6. Set the head aside for now.

Making The Neck:

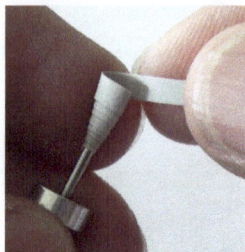

1. Take the 7 inch grey strip and start to roll it into a cone shape.

2. Be sure to glue it at almost every turn you make so it won't come apart on you.

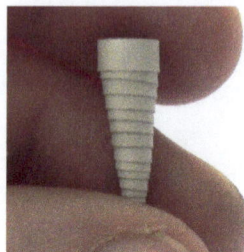

3. You should now have a shape that resembles something like an ice cream cone.

4. When the cone is finished, glue it to the underside of the head.

Making The Body And Wings:

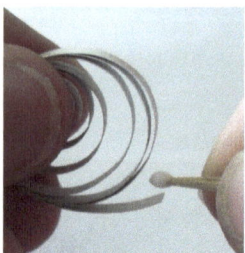

1. Take the 18 inch strip of grey and roll it into a loose coil. Glue the end so that it is a closed coil.

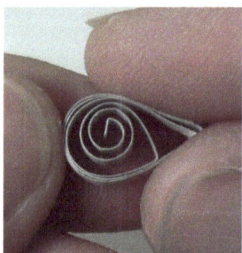

2. Pinch one end of the coil so that it forms a long tear drop shape. This is the body.

3. Take one of the 10 inch strips of blue-grey paper and roll it into a loose coil. Glue the end so that it is a closed coil.

4. Pinch one end of the coil so that it forms a tear drop shape. This is your first wing.

5. Take the second 5 inch strips of blue-grey paper and also roll it into a loose coil. Glue the end so that it is a closed coil.

6. Pinch one end of the coil so that it forms a tear drop shape. This is the second wing.

7. Glue one of the blue-grey tear drop shapes to one side of the grey tear drop shape, making sure that the round edges match up but that the blue-grey piece is angled downward and the two pointed ends do not match up.

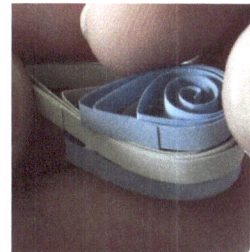

8. Repeat step seven for the second blue-grey tear drop shape on the opposite side of the body.

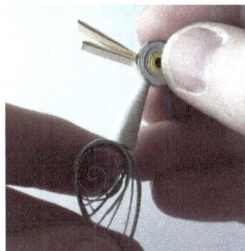

9. Glue the head and neck slightly to one side of the rounded edge of the body and wings.

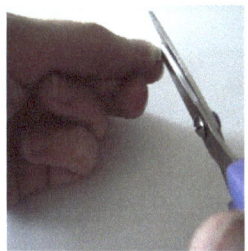

10. Take the 1 inch grey strip and cut one end of it on an angle so that the end comes to a point.

11. Glue the end of the 1 inch strip to the front of the body right where the neck and body meet, with the pointed end of the paper facing down.

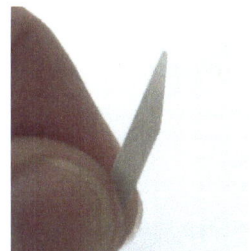

12. Take one of the ½ inch grey strips and cut one end of it on an angle so that the end comes to a point.

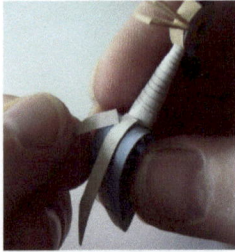

13. Glue the end of the ½ inch strip (point down) to the front of the body right where the neck and body meet, but off to the left just a little bit from where you glued the 1 inch pointed grey strip.

14. Take the second ½ inch grey strips and cut one end of it on an angle so that the end comes to a point.

15. Glue the end of the second ½ inch strip (point down) to the front of the body right where the neck and body meet, but off to the right just a little bit from where you glued the 1 inch pointed grey strip.7

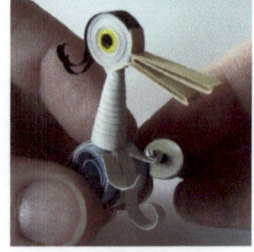

16. Curl all three grey pointed ends upwards towards the head.

Making The Legs:

1. Take the tooth pick and wrap one of the 5 ½ inch yellow strips of paper around it to form a tube roughly 1 inch long. Leave a 1 inch long tail of paper unrolled. If you find that it won't wrap smoothly, that's OK. Just squish down the parts that stick up. It may be a bit rough looking but then a heron's legs aren't smooth anyways.

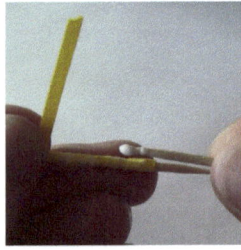

2. When it is wrapped, coat the whole tube with glue and let it dry for a minute or two. Be sure that you don't accidentally glue it right to the toothpick and that it will slide off of your toothpick when you are done.

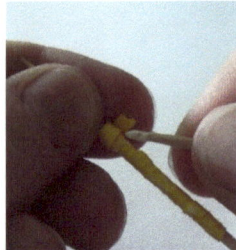

3. When the glue has dried, wrap the remaining 1 inch tail end around the tube in a straight line, two or three times and glue it in place.

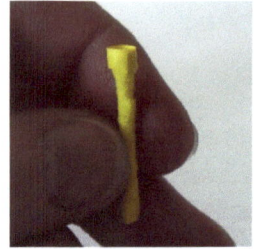

4. Slide the yellow tube off of the toothpick.

** Tip: If you can't get the yellow tube off of the tooth pick then just leave it on and snip off the visible parts of the toothpick with a pair of scissors.

5. Repeat steps one to four for the second 5 ½ inch yellow strip.

6. When both legs have dried, take the ends of the legs that you wrapped two or three times around with the 1 inch tail and cut off a piece on a diagonal angle. (You can skip this step if you want your heron tilting down to look like it's fishing).

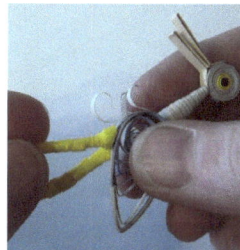

7. Glue both legs to the under side of the Heron's body. If you need to, trim the legs with a pair of scissors so that they are the same length.

Making The Water:

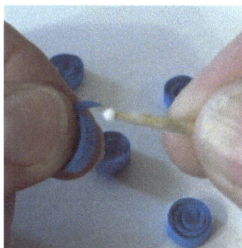

1. The Heron won't be able to stand up without some help. So make him look like he is standing in some water. Start by taking one of your blue strips of 6 inch paper and roll it into a coil with an open center

2. For the first two, be sure the opening is big enough to fit the legs into. It should be a tight fit, but if needed, you can use a tooth pick or pair of pointed tweezers to make the center holes wider.

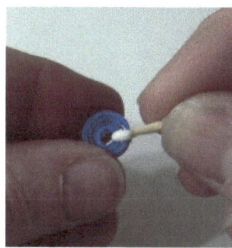

3. Coat the under side of the blue coil with glue and let it dry for a few minutes. Repeat steps one and two for all six of the blue strips.

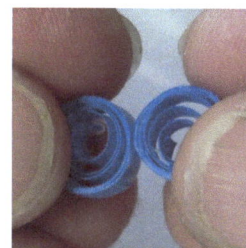

4. Once all six of the coils are made and dry, glue the two that the legs fit into side by side.

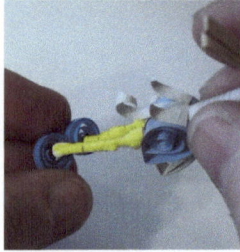

5. Add some glue to the heron's feet and slide them into these two coils.

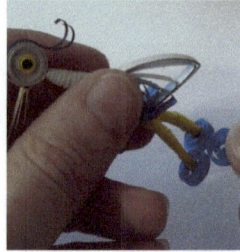

6. Start gluing the other blue coils to the first two. As you add more coils, the heron will begin to balance out and stand on it's own.

7. Additionally, create two or three of the quilled cat tails (instructions found on page 34) and attach them to of a couple of the blue coils to make the heron look like he is standing at the edge of the pond.

Tip: If you find that your heron is still not standing up properly after gluing it to the blue coils, try either 1) adding additional blue coils and gluing them to the side of the first ones for added balance, or 2) make more cat tails and attach all their water bases to the water bases of the heron until he is balanced enough to stand on his own.

You now have a blue heron looking for fish near the waters edge! He will make the perfect gift for all those bird lovers and nature lovers that you know!

Water Lily

Level - Intermediate

You Will Need:

- 4 strips of green 1/16" quilling paper, 18 inches (46 cm) long
- 6 strips of white 1/8" quilling paper, 8 inches (20.5 cm) long
- 3 strips of white 1/8" quilling paper, 3 inches (8 cm) long
- 6 strip of white 1/8" quilling paper, 6 inches (15.5 cm) long
- 1 strip of white 1/8" quilling paper, 3/4 inch (2 cm) long
- 1 strip of yellow 1/8" quilling paper, 1 inch (2.5 cm) long

Directions:

Making The Lily Pad:

1. Roll one of the 18 inch long green strips into a very loose coil. (If you don't have any 1/16" paper you can cut a strip of 1/8" paper lengthwise in two).

2. The coil should be about 3/4" in diameter after it is rolled. Glue the end so that your coil does not come undone.

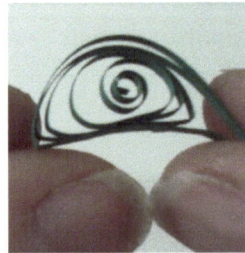

3. Pinch both ends of this coil and give it a bit of a curve so that it looks like a crescent moon.

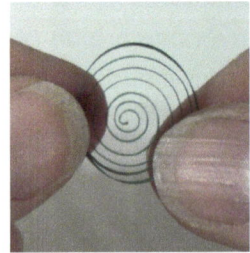

4. Roll a second 18 inch long , 1/16" green strips into a very loose coil.

5. This coil should also be about 3/4" in diameter after it is rolled. Glue the end so that your coil does not come undone.

6. Pinch one end of this coil tight and pinch the other end just gently so that it takes on almost a tear drop like shape.

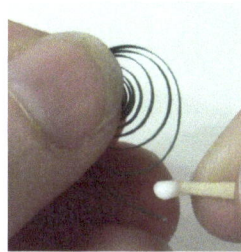

7. Roll a third 18 inch long , 1/16" green strips into a very loose coil, making it slightly smaller (about 1/2" in diameter) and glue the end down.

8. Gently pinch both ends of this coil so that it becomes a Marquise or an eye shape.

9. Take the teardrop and glue the outer curve of it to the inner curve of the crescent.

10. Now take the Marquise and glue one side of it against the teardrop. You will now have one whole shape that looks like a badly misshapen heart.

11. Take the last 18 inch strip and starting from the inside of the V shape of the heart, start to glue and wrap the strip all the way around the shape a couple of times. This is known as banding. This will help to strengthen the edges and will hide the seams where the pieces are joined together.

12. It is during this stage that you can slightly modify your shape, if you feel it doesn't look quite right, by curving it more or pinching it more in places. When you are finished set it aside.

49

Making The Flower:

1. Take one of the 8 inch strips of white and roll it into loose coil.

2. The coil should be just over 1/4" (1 cm) in diameter after it is rolled. Glue the end so that your coil does not come undone.

3. Pinch both ends of the coil so that you have a Marquise shape.

4. Repeat steps one to three until you have completed all 6 of the 8 inch white strips.

5. Glue the 6 white Marquise end to end so that they form a flower or star shape. Set it aside.

6. Take one of the 3 inch white strips and curve both ends in to the center of the strip and glue them in place. It should look like a figure 8 or an infinity symbol.

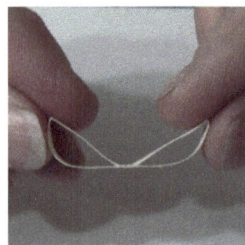

7. Pinch both ends of the figure 8 so that the top edges are straight and the bottom edges are curved. It will look something like the shape of a pair of glasses from the 1950's.

8. Repeat steps 6 and 7 for the other two 3 inch white strips.

9. *Glue one of the figure 8 shapes on to the white flower shape making sure that it lines up with the petals underneath it.*

10. *Crisscross and glue the second figure 8 shape on top of the first one, also making sure that it aligns with the petals directly below it.*

11. *Repeat for the final figure 8 shape then set it aside.*

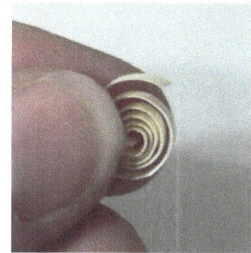

12. *Take one of the 6 inch strips of white and roll it into loose coil. Glue the end so that your coil does not come undone.*

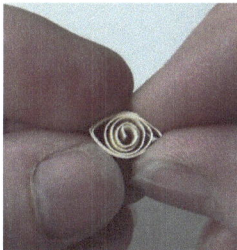

13. *Pinch both ends of the coil so that you have a Marquise shape.*

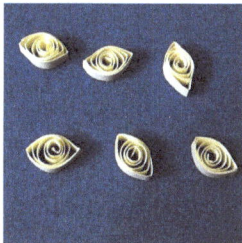

14. *Repeat steps eleven to thirteen until you have completed all six of the 4 inch white strips.*

15. *Glue the six white Marquise in each of the spaces between the figure 8 shapes on the flower. They should be standing on their pointed ends in a diagonal direction pointing up and outwards.*

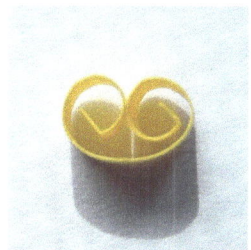

16. *Take the 1 inch yellow strip and coil both ends of the strip in towards each other to make a C scroll.*

17. *Repeat for the second yellow strip.*

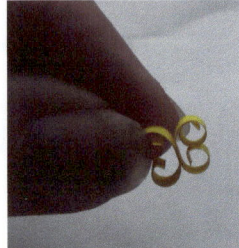

18. *Glue the C scroll strips to each other, back to back.*

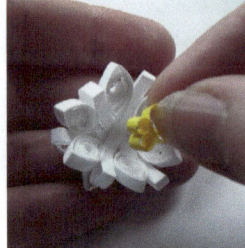

19. *Glue the yellow heart scrolls into the center of the white flower. You have completed the water lily flower.*

20. *Glue the water lily flower on to the green lily pad.*

You now have a water lily! You can use it to create pond scenery or as a place for other quilled creatures such as frogs, butterflies, lady bugs or dragonflies to perch on.

Dragonfly

Level - Intermediate

You Will Need:

- 1 strip of light purple 1/8" quilling paper, 6 inches (15 cm) long
- 2 strips of black 1/16" quilling paper, 1 1/2 inches (4 cm) long
- 2 emerald green rhinestones , 1/8 inch (3mm) in diameter
- 2 strips of iridescent ribbon or paper, 1 inch (3 cm) long, 3/16 inch (5 mm) wide
- 4 strip of black 1/16" quilling paper, 1/2 inch (1 cm) long
- 2 strip of black 1/16" quilling paper, 5/8 inch (1.5 cm) long

Directions:

Making The Body:

If you've already made the snail in this book then you will know that making the body for this can be a little bit tricky.

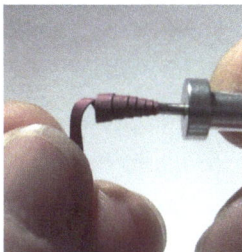 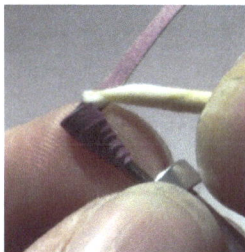 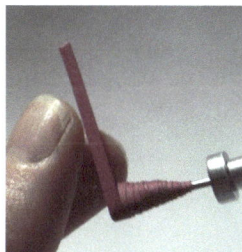 

1. Take the 6 inch strip of light purple and roll it into a cone shape. As it gets longer the cone will start to naturally curve a little bit. That is OK, it is supposed to do that.

2. Be sure to glue it at almost every turn you make or it will quickly come apart on you.

3. Continue to roll and glue until you have only about an inch or so of paper left then stop and make sure everything is glued up to that point.

4. Now fold the end over the opening so that it starts to cover the opening, making it narrower. It will not fully cover the opening, but it doesn't need to.

5. Glue the piece that you have just folded over to the edge on the opposite side of the cone.

6. Cut off any excess paper that remains.

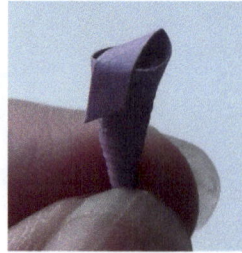

7. You should now have a shape that resembles something like an odd shaped ice cream cone with an oval shaped opening.

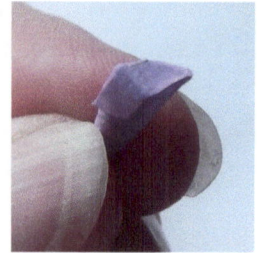

8. Glue the edges of the opening, pinch it shut and push it flat a little so that you no longer see any opening.

Making The Eyes:

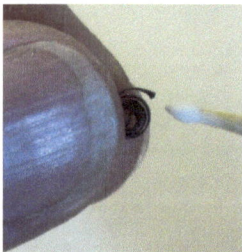

1. Take one of the 1 1/2 inches (4 cm) long black strips and roll it into a loose coil. Glue the end so that your coil does not come undone.

2. Glue the coil to the larger end of the light purple cone shape along one side.

3. Make a loose coil from the second 1 1/2 inches (4 cm) long black strip and glue it beside the first black coil on the body.

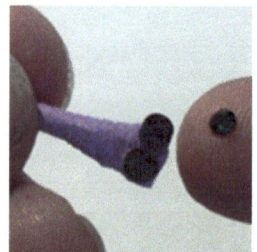

4. Glue the two emerald coloured rhinestones to the top of each of the black coils.

Making The Wings:

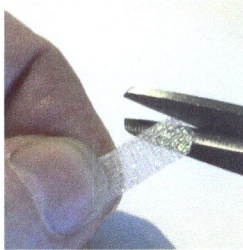

1. Take one of the iridescent strips of ribbon or paper and with some scissors, round the corners off of both ends. These are the wings.

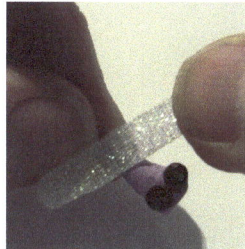

2. Glue the wing on a diagonal angle onto the back of the body, just behind the eyes.

3. Repeat for the second iridescent strip, gluing it on top of the first one in a crisscross shape.

Making The Legs:

1. Take one of the strips of black 1/16" quilling paper, 1/2 inch (1 cm) long and fold a small piece of one end over to make a foot. It may be easier to do this with a pair of tweezers.

2. Curve the other end just slightly in the opposite direction that the foot is folded in so that your piece looks kind of like the shape of a number 2.

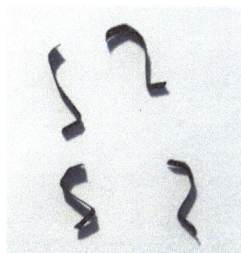

3. Repeat steps 1 and 2 for each of the other three black 1/2 inch (1 cm) long strips.

4. Glue the curved ends of the black strips to bottom of the purple body just below the wings to give your dragonfly four legs.

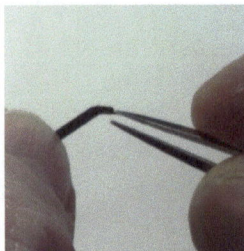

5. Take one of the strips of black 1/16" quilling paper, 5/8 inch (1.5 cm) long and fold a small piece of one end over to make a foot.

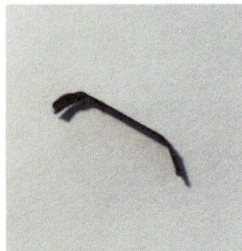

6. Curve the other end just slightly in the same direction that the foot is folded in.

7. Repeat steps 5 and 6 for the other strip of 5/8 inch (1.5 cm) long black quilling paper.

8. Glue the curved ends of the black strips under the purple body just below the eyes. Angle them so that they are sticking out almost horizontally from the body and it looks like he wants to give someone a hug. They should protrude out past the head a little bit. Once the glue is completely dry you may need to turn them and adjust them a little bit with a pair of tweezers.

You now have a little dragonfly! The sparkle of his eyes and wings are sure to catch peoples attention in whatever project you use him for!

Mosquito

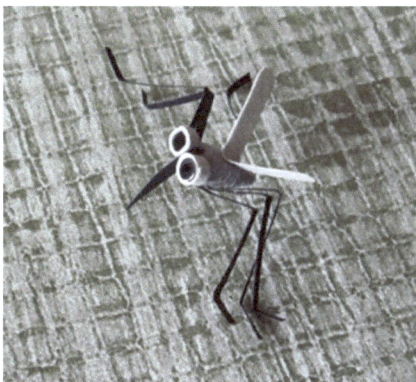

Level - Intermediate

You Will Need:

- 2 strips of black 1/16 " quilling paper, 1 inch (2.5 cm) long
- 2 strips of light grey 1/16" quilling paper, 2 inches (5 cm) long
- 1 strip of black 1/16" quilling paper, 3/4 inch (2 cm) long
- 1 strip of medium grey 1/8" quilling paper, 5 inches (13 cm) long
- 1 strip of light grey 1/8" quilling paper, 1 inch (2.5 cm) long
- 3 strips of black 1/16" quilling paper, 1 inch (2.5 cm) long

Directions:

Making The Head:

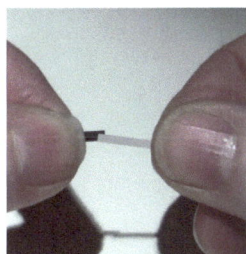

1. Glue one of the black 1 inch strips to the end of one of the light grey 2 inch strips. You now have one longer strip going from black to grey.

2. Roll that strip into a tight coil.

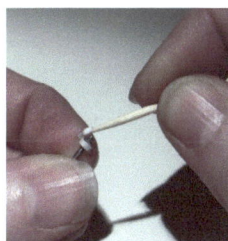

3. Glue the end in place so it does not unravel on you. This is the mosquitoes eye.

4. Repeat steps 1 to 3 to create the second eye.

57

5. *Take one of the 1 inch black strips and cut one end of it on a diagonal angle so that it comes to a point. This is the stinger (known scientifically as the proboscis).*

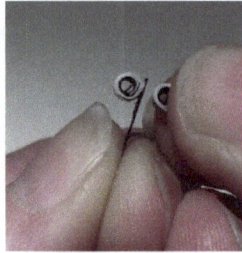

6. *Glue both eyes, one on each side of the proboscis so that the point is at the far end.*

7. *Set it aside to dry.*

Making The Body:

1. *Take the 5 inch medium grey strip and start to roll it into a cone shape.*

2. *Be sure to glue it at almost every turn you make or it will quickly come apart on you.*

3. *You should now have a shape that resembles something like an ice cream cone. Pinch the open end just a little bit so that the opening is an oval shape instead of a round shape.*

4. *When the cone is finished, glue the head to the end with the oval opening.*

Making The Wings:

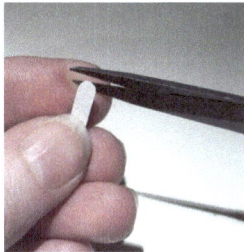

1. Take the light grey 1 inch strip of paper and with some scissors, round the corners off of both ends.

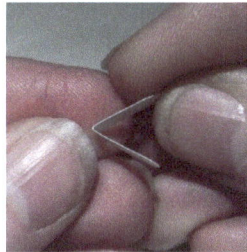

2. Once the ends are rounded, fold it in half. These are the wings.

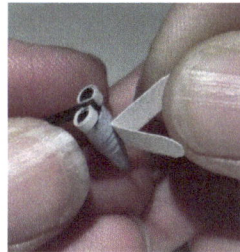

3. Glue the wings to the top of the body, behind the eyes.

4. Set it aside to dry.

Making The Legs:

1. Cut all 3 of the black 1 inch, 1/16th wide strips in half length wise, straight down the middle, being careful not to cut them right off. You should now have 6 very thin black strips of paper.

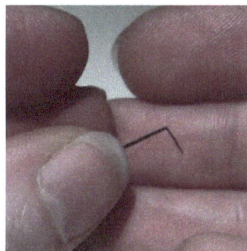

2. Take one strip of the black paper you have just cut and make a fold at one end about 1/8th inch (3mm) long.

3. Make a second fold in the opposite direction about 5/8th inch (15mm) from the first fold.

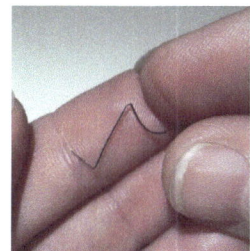

4. Curve the paper just a little in the opposite direction from the second fold. This is a leg.

5. *Repeat steps 1 to 4 for all six of the legs.*

6. *Glue the legs to the under belly of the mosquito.*

** Tip: If the legs seem to be " too fiddly" to work with, try using 3 strips that are 2 inches long instead of 6 that are 1 inch long (make all the folds in the same places). As well, if you don't like how the legs look under the body, you could try using a small piece of medium grey paper to cover the area where they join together.

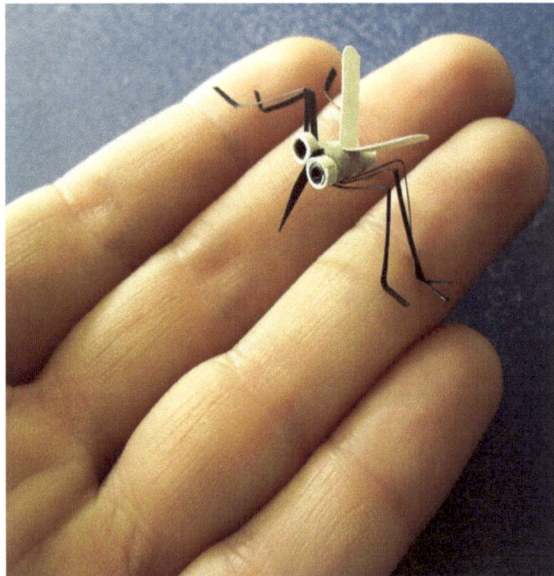

You now have a little mosquito! Go ahead and make some more. The paper versions are much more fun than the real thing!

Swimming Turtle

Level - Intermediate

You Will Need:

- 2 strips of medium brown 1/8" quilling paper, 18 inches (46 cm) long
- 2 strips of green 1/8" quilling paper, 6 inches (15.5 cm) long
- 2 strips of green 1/8" quilling paper, 3 inches (8 cm) long
- 1 strip of green 1/8" quilling paper, 5 inches (13 cm) long
- 1 strip of black 1/16" quilling paper, 1 inches (2.5 cm) long
- 7 strips of light brown 1/8" quilling paper, 3/8th inches (1 cm) long
- A pair of tweezers

Directions:

Making The Shell:

1. Roll one of the 18 inch medium brown strips into a tight solid coil.

2. Glue the end so that your coil does not come undone.

3. Add the second 18 inch medium brown strip to the end of where the first coil finished and glue it in place.

4. Continue to roll the 18 inch medium brown strip around the coil to make it even bigger and then glue the end in place.

5. With your fingers, carefully push the center of the brown coil out until it forms a dome. This will be your turtle shell.

6. Coat the inner side of the dome with glue so that it won't fall apart.

7. Set it aside and let it dry.

Making The Legs:

1. Roll one of the 6 inch green strips into a loose coil.

2. Glue the end in place so it does not unravel on you.

3. Pinch one end of the coil so that it forms a tear drop shape.

4. Repeat steps one through three for the second 6 inch strip.

5. Roll one of the 3 inch green strips into a loose coil and glue the end in place so it does not unravel on you.

6. Pinch one end of the coil so that it forms a tear drop shape.

7. Repeat steps five through seven for the second 3 inch strip. You should now have four tear drop shapes; two big ones and two little ones.

8. Glue the four tear drop shapes to the under side of the turtle shell with the two larger ones positioned up near where the head will go and the two smaller ones positioned at the back end of the turtle.

Making The Head:

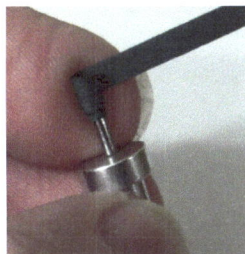

1. Take the 5 inch strip of green and start to roll it into a cone shape.

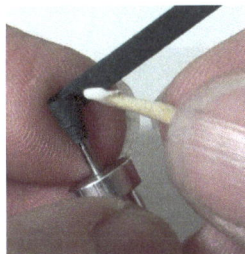

2. Be sure to glue it at almost every turn you make or it will quickly come apart on you. Continue to roll and glue until you have only about an inch or so of paper left then stop and make sure everything is glued up to that point.

3. Fold the 1 inch long end over so that it starts to cover the opening and glue the end to the edge on the opposite side of the cone. It will not fully cover the opening, but it doesn't need to yet.

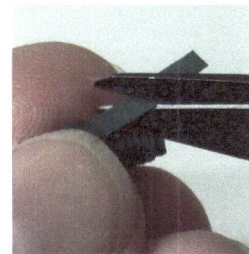

4. Cut off any excess paper that remains.

Making The Eyes:

5. Add glue to any openings you may find at the end of the cone.

6. With a pair of tweezers, squeeze together the glued openings so that they are no longer open.

7. You now have the head of your turtle. If the wider end of the cone seems to have too much   of a point to it, you can always push the point in a little to round it out somewhat.

8. Glue the head to the underside of the turtle shell between the larger front two legs.

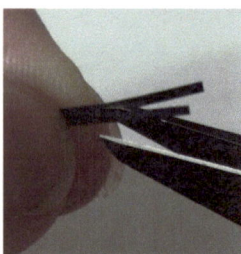

1. Take the 1 inch strip of black 1/16th quilling paper and cut it length wise up the middle so that you have two pieces.

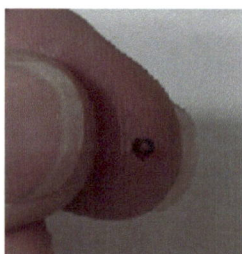

2. Roll both of the black pieces into a tight coil. These will be it's eyes.

3. With a pair of tweezers, carefully glue the eyes onto either side of the head.

1. Take the seven strips of light brown paper and glue them so that they over lap each other side by side. Once they are glued together they will resemble a wooden bridge.

2. Trim and round the sides with a pair of scissors, leaving the ends straight.

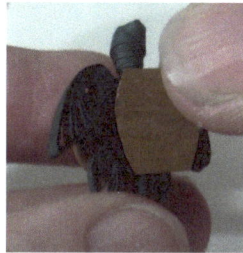

3. Glue the under belly to the underside of the turtle.

4. The under belly is not needed if you are gluing it onto card stock, but as a 3-D project it really finishes off the look of the turtle.

You now have a swimming turtle! You can make more for your pond project or you can go on to make a standing turtle.

Standing Turtle

Level – Intermediate

You Will Need:

- 2 strips of medium brown 1/8" quilling paper, 18 inches (46 cm) long
- 1 strip of green 1/8" quilling paper, 5 inches (13 cm) long
- 1 strip of black 1/16" quilling paper, 1 inches (2.5 cm) long
- 1 strip of green 1/8" quilling paper, ¼ inch (6mm) long
- 7 strips of light brown 1/8" quilling paper, 3/8th inches (1 cm) long
- 8 strips of green 1/8" quilling paper, 8 inches (20.5 cm) long
- A pair of tweezers

Directions:

Making The Shell:

1. Roll the 18 inch brown strip into a tight solid coil.

2. Glue the end so that your coil does not come undone.

3. Add the second 18 inch brown strip to the end of where the coil finished and glue it in place.

4. Continue to roll the 18 inch brown strip around the coil to make it even bigger and then glue the end in place.

66

5. *With your fingers, carefully push the center of the brown coil out until it forms a dome. This will be your turtle shell.*

6. *Coat the inner side of the dome with glue so that it won't fall apart.*

7. *Set it aside and let it dry.*

Making The Head:

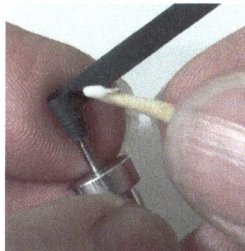

1. *Take the 5 inch strip of green and start to roll it into a cone shape.*

2. *Be sure to glue it at almost every turn you make or it will quickly come apart on you. Continue to roll and glue until you have only about an inch or so of paper left then stop and make sure everything is glued up to that point.*

3. *Now fold the end over the opening so that it starts to cover the opening, making it narrower and glue it to the edge on the opposite side of the cone. It will not fully cover the opening, but it doesn't need to yet.*

4. *Cut off any excess paper that remains.*

5. Add glue to any openings you may find at the end of the cone.

6. With a pair of tweezers, squeeze together the glued openings so that they are no longer open.

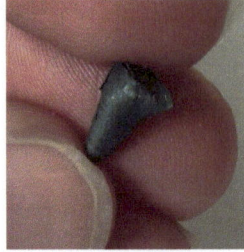

7. You now have the head of your turtle. If the wider end of the cone seems to have too much   of a point to it, you can always push the point in a little to round it out somewhat.

8. Glue the neck to the underside of the turtle shell.

Making The Eyes:

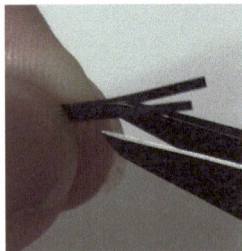

1. Take the 1 inch strip of black 1/16th quilling paper and cut it length wise up the middle so that you have two pieces.

2. Roll both of the black pieces into a tight coil. These will be it's eyes.

3. With a pair of tweezers, carefully glue the eyes onto either side of the head.

Making The Tail:

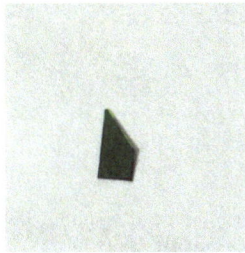

1. Take the ¼ inch strip of green and cut one end on a diagonal angle so that it comes to a point.

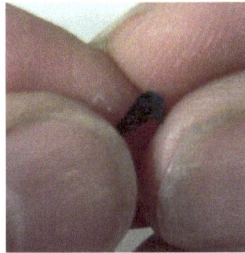

2. At the opposite side, fold a tiny bit of the end over.

3. Glue the tail to the under side of the turtle shell at the opposite end from where the head sits.

Making The Under Belly:

1. Take the seven strips of light brown paper and glue them so that they over lap each other side by side. Once they are glued together they will resemble a wooden bridge.

2. Trim and round the sides with a pair of scissors, leaving the ends straight.

3. Glue the under belly to the underside of the turtle.

4. It will go over top of the neck and the base of the tail. You may need to trim it a little more with the scissors once it is glued on.

1. *Take one of the 8 inch green strips and roll it into a tight coil. Glue the end so that it does not come undone.*

2. *With the rest of the 8 inch green strips make seven more of these tight coils.*

3. *Glue two of the tight coils together, one on top of the other. This will be a leg.*

4. *Continue gluing the coils together two at a time until you have four legs and then glue the legs to the under belly of the turtle.*

You now have a standing turtle to join in on the fun with your swimming turtles!

Beaver

Level - Intermediate

You Will Need:

- 2 strips of light brown ¼" quilling paper, 24 inches (61 cm) long
- 2 strips of light brown 1/8" quilling paper, ½ inch (12 mm) long
- 1 strip of light brown 1/8" quilling paper, 10 inches (25.5 cm) long
- 4 strips of dark brown 1/8" quilling paper, 1 inches (2.5 cm) long
- 4 strips of medium brown 1/8" quilling paper, 1 inches (2.5 cm) long
- 2 strips of light brown 1/8" quilling paper, ¼ inch (7 mm) long
- 1 strips of white 1/8" quilling paper, 1/8 inch (3 mm) long

Directions:

Making The Body:

1. Roll the first 24 inch light brown strip into a tight solid coil.

2. Glue the end so that your coil does not come undone.

3. Add the second 24 inch light brown strip to the end of where the coil finished and glue it in place.

4. Continue to roll the light brown strip around the coil to make it even bigger and then glue the end in place.

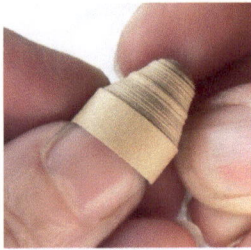

5. Carefully push
the center of the
coil out until it
forms a dome. If
you find that your
fingers are too big
to do this, try using
the eraser end of a
pencil. This will be
the body of your
beaver.

6. Coat the inner
side of the dome
with glue so that it
won't fall apart.

7. Set it aside and
let it dry.

Making The Ears:

1. Take one of the
½ inch light brown
strips and roll it
into a loose coil.

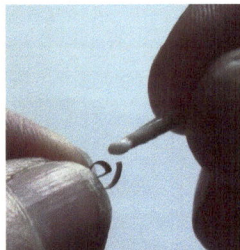

2. Glue the end so
that your open coil
does not come
undone.

3. Take the second
½ inch light brown
strip and roll it into
an open coil. Glue
the end of this coil
also.

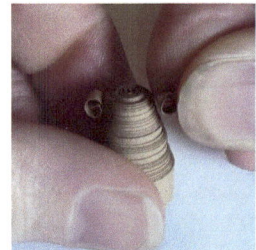

4. Glue both open
coils onto each
side of the body.

Making The Muzzle:

1. Take the 10 inch light brown strip and roll it into a tight coil. Glue the end so that your loose coil does not come undone.

2. With the eraser end of a pencil or the end of your quilling tool, carefully push the center of the light brown coil out until it forms a small dome.

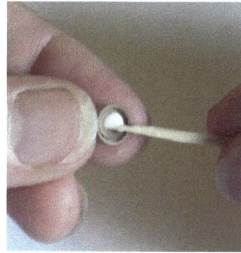

3. Coat the inner side of the dome with glue so that it won't fall apart.

4. Glue the dome onto the body between the two ears. Set it aside to dry.

Making The Tail:

1. Take the four 1 inch strips of medium brown and the four 1 inch strips of dark brown and weave them together in a checker board pattern.

2. Be sure to glue it where almost every strip overlaps. Try to make sure the strips are close together and that there aren't any spaces between the strips.

3. Once they are woven together, take a pair of scissors and cut the weave into a tear drop shape.

4. Glue the tail onto the body on one side so that it sticks out and you can see it from the front of the body.

73

Making The Paws:

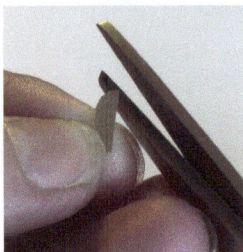

1. Take one of the two light brown ¼ inch strips and cut one end so that it is rounded.

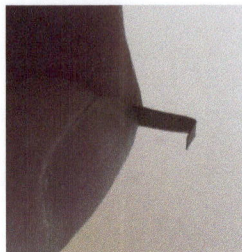

2. Fold the opposite end just enough to give it a place to add some glue.

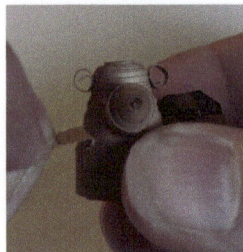

3. Glue the paw onto the body just below and off to one side of the muzzle.

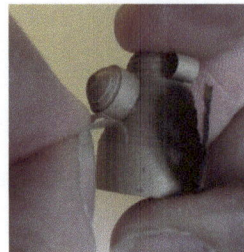

4. Repeat steps one to three for the other paw.

Making The Teeth:

1. Take the 1/8 inch strip of white and cut it in half.

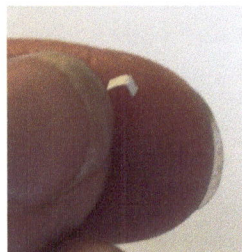

2. Make a tiny fold at one end of one piece; just enough to give it a place to add some glue.

3. Glue the tooth to the underside of the muzzle. Repeat steps 1 to 3 for the other tooth.

4. Now just add some eyes either with a marker or some bits of black paper or some tiny black rhinestones.

Now you have a little beaver ready to work hard at making your paper crafts look fabulous!

BONUS: Additional Instructions for fallen logs

Making The Stump:

You Will Need:

- *1 strip of light brown ¼" quilling paper, 14 inches (35.5cm) long*
- *1 strip of dark brown ¼" quilling paper, 1 inch (2.5 cm) long*

   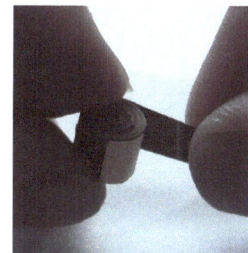

1. Roll the 14 inch long light brown strip into a tight solid coil.

2. Glue the end so that your coil does not come undone.

3. You will have a round circle with rings in the center that look like tree rings.

4. Take the 1 inch strip of dark brown and wrap it around the outside of the tight coil, gluing it into place. This is the bark for the stump.

Making The Fallen Logs:

‣ 2 strips of light brown ¼" quilling paper, 4 inches (10 cm) long
‣ 2 strips of dark brown ¼" inch quilling paper, ½ inches (1.5 cm) long

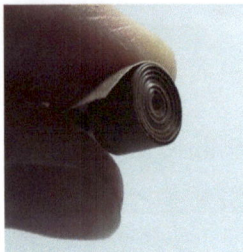

1. Roll the 4 inch light brown strip into a tight solid coil.

2. Glue the end so that your coil does not come undone.

3. Repeat step 1 and 2 for the second log.

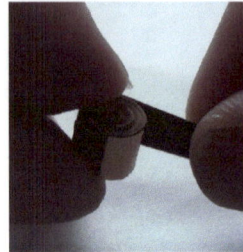

4. Take the ½ inch strips of dark brown and wrap them around the outside of the tight coils, gluing them into place. This is the bark for the logs.

Making The Tree Branches:

You Will Need:

‣ 1 strip of dark brown 1/8 inch quilling paper, 3 inches (8 cm) long
‣ 1 strip of green 1/8 inch quilling paper, ¼ inches (1 cm) long

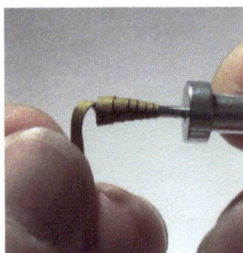

1. Take the 3 inch strip of dark brown and roll it into a cone shape.

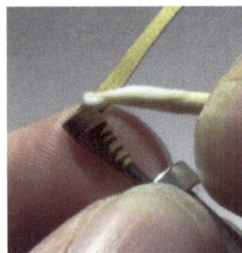

2. Glue it at every turn so it won't come apart on you.

3. Cut the green strip into 3 leaf shapes.

4. Glue the leaves onto the branch which ever way you like.

Adding the fallen tree branches makes your beaver look like he is hard at work.

Tadpole

Level – Easy

You Will Need:

- *2 strips of medium brown 1/8 inch quilling paper, 3 ½ inches (9 cm) long*
- *1 strip of medium brown 1/8 inch quilling paper, ½ inches (1.5 cm) long*

Directions:

Making The Body:

 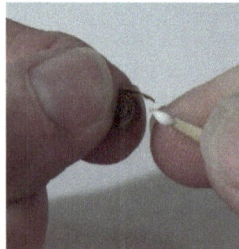  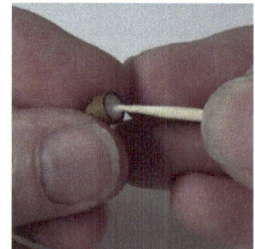

1. Roll one of the the 3 ½ inch medium brown strips into a tight solid coil.

2. Glue the end so that your coil does not come undone.

3. With your quilling tool or tooth pick, carefully push the center of the medium brown coil out until it forms a dome.

4. Coat the inner side of the dome with glue so that it won't fall apart.

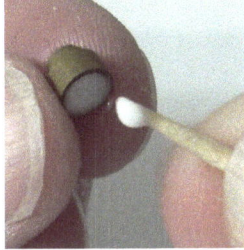

5. Repeat steps 1 to 4 for the second 3 ½ inch strip.

6. Glue the two domes together so that it looks like a pill shape. This is the body.

Making The Tail:

1. Cut one end of the ½ inch strip on a diagonal angle.

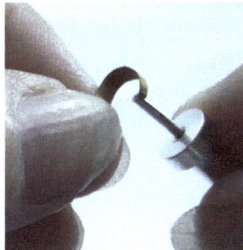

2. Curl the strip into an 'S' shape.

3. Glue the tail onto the body.

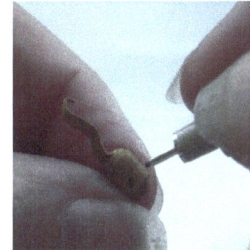

4. With a felt tip pen draw on some eyes.

With a few more tadpoles you can have a whole frog family!

ABOUT THE AUTHOR

Dana Woodard was born and raised in North Bay, Ontario, Canada. She was first introduced to quilling when she was a teenager by her mother who showed her how to make some beautiful snowflake Christmas decorations. She only just dabbled in quilling and over the years she set it aside and forgot about it.

Then she met Moira Hiscock who re-introduced the craft to her and once again she was hooked. This time not only did she craft from the designs of other wonderful authors but she started to come up with her own designs. After showing them to Moira and Moira's friend Betty, the idea of creating a book to share her designs with other paper quillers was born.

As the designs were thought up and filled the pages, she realized that she had more designs than expected and already began plans to create a second and even a third book.

Like most crafters, Dana is interested in more than one craft. She also enjoys Iris folding, needle felting, card making, polymer clay, drawing and sewing. She is never bored because she always has some craft or other on the go or is learning something new.

www.ingramcontent.com/pod-product-compliance
Lightning Source LLC
Chambersburg PA
CBHW061054090426
42742CB00002B/42